This book
belongs to:

....

....

When my parents
forgot how to be friends

Text: *Jennifer Moore-Mallinos*

Illustrations: *Marta Fàbrega*

BARRON'S

My parents used to be friends. We did everything together. Every Saturday was a special family night. We were always laughing, and it was so much fun. Sometimes we played board games, and other times we watched a movie and ate popcorn. No matter what we did, it was always together.

I knew my parents were forgetting how to be friends because things started to change. Sometimes I would wake up late at night and hear my parents arguing. I didn't know what they were arguing about, but they seemed very mad, and my Mom usually cried.

Whenever this happened, I would hide under my blanket or pillow, hoping the yelling would stop. Even though the shouting got louder and I could still hear my Mom cry, hiding made me feel better.

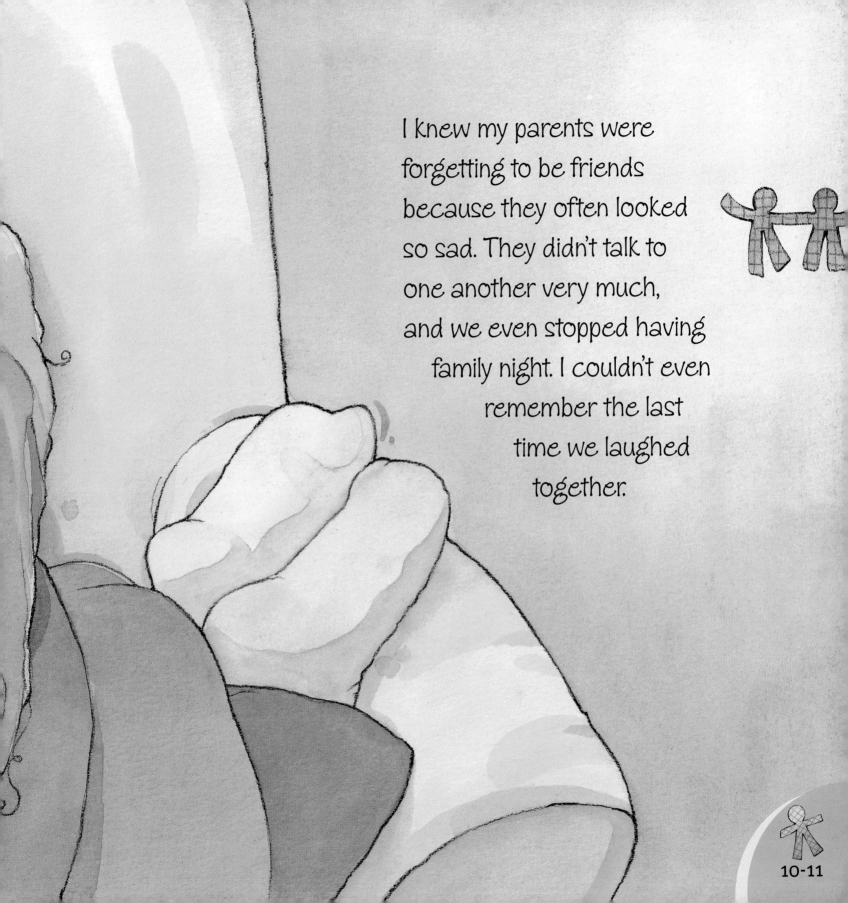

I knew my parents were forgetting to be friends because they often looked so sad. They didn't talk to one another very much, and we even stopped having family night. I couldn't even remember the last time we laughed together.

Sometimes I would find my Mom sitting alone in her bedroom, quietly crying. She looked so lonely. I didn't know what to do to make her feel better, so I'd give her a hug and that seemed to work, because she stopped crying.

Now I knew for sure that my parents were not friends anymore, because my Dad packed his suitcase and moved away. He now lives by himself in a house in town. When Dad left, he gave me a big hug. He told me that he loved me and that he would see me soon.

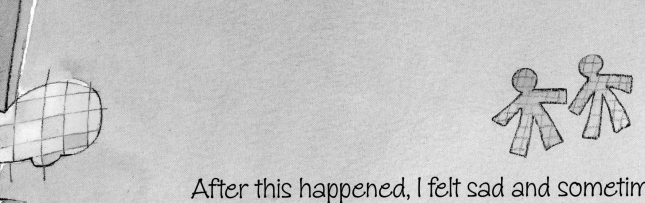

After this happened, I felt sad and sometimes I thought it was my fault. Maybe if I was a better listener or did better at school, my parents would be friends again? My Mom and Dad kept telling me it was not my fault that they forgot how to be friends. I believed them, but sometimes I would wonder if maybe it was my fault.

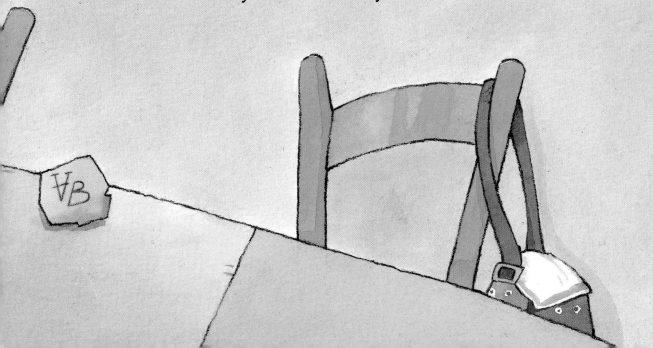

Mom and Dad explained to me that sometimes parents got along better when they lived in different houses. They both said that no matter where they lived, they would always love me and be there for me.

They were right! After my Dad moved to a different house, things started to change.

My Mom and Dad didn't look as sad as they did before.
This made me feel better and much happier.

Even though I live in my house with my Mom, I call my Dad on the phone as many times as I want and visit him every week. Sometimes I stay overnight at Dad's house, and it's so much fun. We like to play games or read together. The best part is that we laugh a lot.

On special occasions, like my birthday, Dad comes over to my house so we can have a family night together. It's just like old times! We play board games or watch a movie. We even laugh together. My Mom and Dad may not live in the same house, but we are still a family, and our time together seems extra special.

 Now I understand that even though my parents forgot how to be friends, it doesn't mean they don't love me or that they stop being my parents. The time I spend with each of my parents is special. We're not all together, but we all seem happier. The arguing has finally stopped.

My Mom and Dad will always love me and
are always bugging me to do my homework.
They take turns picking me up from school,
and whenever I have a basketball game, they
are both there to cheer me on! I love my
Mom and my Dad. They are the best!

Note
to parents

Growing up in a one-parent family was certainly tough! As a child I did not understand the dynamics of the situation or the struggles which led to my parents' decision to live apart. Initially, I blamed myself for my parents' behavior. I would spend countless hours trying to figure out what "I" had done to contribute to my family's difficulties.

I still remember the day when my mom sat me down and took the time to explain to me what had happened in our family. That was the day that many of my fears and anxieties were alleviated. Not only did I learn what to expect from my parents and of the situation as a whole, but most importantly I learned that my parents' decision to live apart was not my fault.

Given my personal experience as well as my work with families in my role as a social worker, I recognize and appreciate a child's need to seek understanding in regards to his/her family's situation. Every child has the right to be heard and his/her feelings to be respected.

The purpose of "When My Parents Forgot How To Be Friends" is to acknowledge some of the concerns and anxieties your child may experience during this transition of change within your family unit. Allowing your child the opportunity to explore his/her feelings and fears is the first step in the process of healing. Giving your child the chance to heal by addressing some of these issues, will encourage him/her to become a survivor of separation and divorce, rather than remaining a victim.

This book can also be used as a tool to initiate dialogue and to stimulate communication between you and your children. Your children will be reminded that they are not responsible for the difficulties within the family and that their behavior had no impact on your decision to separate.

Taking the time to read to your child is a wonderful way to share a moment together. Children are important, and what they think and how they feel matters. Let's do our part to show our children that we truly care!

First edition for the United States and Canada
published in 2005 by Barron's Educational Series, Inc.
Original title of the book in Spanish: *Cuando Mis
Padres se Olvidaron de Ser Amigos*
© Copyright 2005 by Gemser Publications S.L.
C/Castell, 38; Teià (08329) Barcelona,
Spain (World Rights)
Author: Jennifer Moore-Mallinos
Illustrator: Marta Fàbrega

All inquiries should be addressed to:
Barron's Educational Series, Inc.
250 Wireless Boulevard
Hauppauge, New York 11788
http://www.barronseduc.com

ISBN-13: 978-0-7641-3172-1
ISBN-10: 0-7641-3172-9
Library of Congress Catalog Card Number 2004112881

Manufactured by L. Rex Printing Company Limited, Hong Kong, China
Date of Manufacture: September 2010
9 8 7 6